CLASSIC DEVOTIONS

A THIRTEEN-WEEK DEVOTIONAL AND INTRODUCTION
TO CLASSIC THEOLOGIANS AND MYSTICS OF
CHRISTIAN HISTORY

CHRISTOPHER J. FREET

Energion Publications
Gonzalez, Florida
2023

ISBN: 978-1-63199-860-7
eISBN 978-1-63199-861-4
Library of Congress Control Number: 2023933832

Energion Publications
P. O. Box 841
Gonzalez, FL 32560

energion.com
pubs@energion.com

TABLE OF CONTENTS

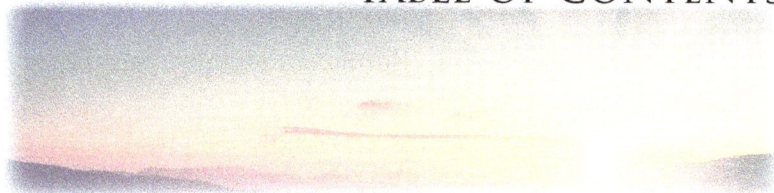

This book is dedicated to:
Joshua Nolt
The time spent together during our monthly retreat days
was so life-giving to me.
I'm forever grateful for the time in silence, prayer, sharing
meals together
and encouraging one another in the Lord.

My Lord and my God,
You are good above all that is good.
You alone are most high, most mighty,
most sufficient, most complete;
You alone are full of sweetness,
of comfort, of beauty and love;
You alone are exalted and glorious above all things;
and in you all good things have their perfect existence,
as they always have done and as they always shall.
Therefore I am not satisfied in anything You give me
that is not Yourself,
nor by any promise or revelation
that does not let me see You or receive You fully.
My heart cannot really rest or find full satisfaction
unless it rests in You.
Thomas a Kempis (*The Imitation of Christ*, Book 3, XXI)

INTRODUCTION

The purpose of this devotional is twofold. First and foremost, to help fellow Christ-followers keep their hearts and minds focused on Jesus Christ, our Lord, Savior and Prince of Peace (cf. Heb. 3:1; 12:2). Secondly, I hope to introduce fellow believers to the rich writings of the classic Christian theologians.

All too often I fear that many Christians are not connected to the "great cloud of witnesses" that have gone before us. Our faith, while being personal on one level, is also corporate on another level. This corporate faith includes all those who have gone before us, from the time of God interacting with Abram until this present day. The Christian story is one of God interacting throughout history with His people. This includes the classic theologians and mystics that many of us are often only loosely acquainted with at best.

This devotional will merely introduce the reader to the classic theologians beginning with the Desert Fathers and Mothers of the fourth century and bringing the reader up to the twentieth century with a look at St. Therese of Lisieux and Thomas Kelly. Part of my hope is that the reader will find their curiosity piqued as they read and perhaps desire to dig deeper into one or more of these classic writings. As such, I have placed a full bibliography at the end of this devotional for those interested in reading further. Of course, while it is important to be familiar with and gain a basic understanding of the Christian classics, the ultimate goal lies elsewhere. Each of these classic theologians had their hearts and minds fixed on Jesus Christ. Union with Christ and growth in godliness or sanctification must always be the vision for the Christ-follower. It is my prayer that this devotional will work toward this end for the glory of God and His kingdom.

One final note, it is important for us to remember that theology and doctrine are never developed apart from the life lived for Christ. As Paul spoke and Luke records in the book of Acts, "This was not done in a corner" (Acts 26:26). Each of these classic authors is writing from within their own context, amidst their own issues and dealing with the events of their own time. This cannot be missed if we are to connect with and understand these writings today. As Richard Woods reminds us, "all authentic spirituality is first of all the product of life, not merely or even primarily of study. The Word became flesh and blood, not paper and ink."[1]

To God be the glory.

---

1   Richard J. Woods, *Christian Spirituality: God's Presence through the Ages* (Orbis: Maryknoll, 2006) pg. xviii.

HOW TO USE THIS DEVOTIONAL

The material in this devotional is designed to be brief. The hope is that the reader would utilize the spiritual discipline of meditation. The first day of each week introduces the theologian(s) that is the focus for that week. Over the next five days, there will be a quote or short passage from that theologian's writings. These writings will be paired up with a Scripture verse or passage. The idea is to meditate upon the writing and the Scripture together. One possible way the time could be spent is as follows:

Silence—acknowledge the Lord's presence is with you.

Read the Devotional Material for the Day—read each day's material three times, slowly.

Silence—Wat is God's invitation for you today?

Pray—Based on what you read and heard, pray it back to the Lord.

The final day of each week contains questions related to the weekly readings. Take time to prayerfully ponder and respond to these questions.

Furthermore, this practice can most certainly be handled at the individual level. I would make the recommendation, however, to take this thirteen-week journey with a small group of other like-minded individuals. Agree to start the material at the same time and gather together for prayer and discussion on the final day of each week. The Christian journey is not meant to be walked alone.

May God bless you on your journey.

THE DESERT FATHERS AND MOTHERS

The rise of the Desert Fathers and Mothers was a very interesting time in Christian history. The two major bases of theology, Alexandria and Antioch, were essentially competing for theological prominence. Also, the late third and early fourth century of the Church found itself in a much more acceptable position in some regards. For example, the rise of Emperor Constantine brought with it the rule the Christianity was now an acceptable religion to practice within the Empire. This largely resulted in the cessation of the persecution of Christians throughout the Roman Empire. This decision would have far-reaching impact throughout the many years of Christian tradition yet to come. This brought about, essentially, the rise of Monasticism.

> Monasticism arose not in response to persecution, but in its absence. Men and women intent on proving their love of God to the point of death 'withdrew' from urban centers and turned to the natural and psychological testing ground of the spirit—the deserts of Egypt, Syria and Palestine. Some saw their encounter with the world, the flesh, and the devil as a life-long combat, others as a foretaste of the life of heaven. However they envisioned it, these primitive monks and nuns established a form of life that would leave an indelible impression upon Christian spirituality until the end of time.[2]

The first recorded monastic was a hermit named Antony. He was a young and wealthy farmer from Egypt. Sometime around the year 270, Antony heard the gospel, specifically the account of the rich young ruler, and took the words to heart. In response,

---

2 Woods, *Christian Spirituality*, 62-3.

Antony sold all of his land and possessions and subsequently left the village where he lived for the desert.[3]

While the early monastics were seeking a life of solitude with God, over time they eventually formed and lived together in communities. These communities were guided by a "rule" and often involved a strict aesthetic lifestyle that moved between solitude, prayer and silence as well as manual labor, outreach and service to the poor and disenfranchised.

WEEK 1, DAY 2

Chapter V

Abbot Pastor said: There are two things which a monk ought to hate above all, for by hating them he can become free in this world. And a brother asked: What are these things? The elder replied: An easy life and vain glory.[4]

John 17:14b-16

"...for they are not of the world any more than I am of the world. My prayer is not that you take them out of the world but that you protect them from the evil one. They are not of the world, even as I am not of it."

---

3   Ibid, 63.
4   All selections from the Desert Fathers and Mothers are taken from: Thomas Merton trans., *The Wisdom of the Desert* (Boston: Shambhala Publications, 1960).

Week 1, Day 3

Chapter XXI

A monk ran into a party of handmaids of the Lord on a certain journey. Seeing them he left the road and gave them a wide berth. But the Abbess said to him: If you were a perfect monk, you would not even have looked close enough to see that we were women.

Matthew 6:22-23

"The eye is the lamp of the body. If your eyes are healthy, your whole body will be full of light. But if your eyes are unhealthy, your whole body will be full of darkness. If then the light within you is darkness, how great is that darkness!"

Week 1, Day 4

Chapter XXV

Abbott Pastor said: The virtue of a monk is made manifest by temptations.

James 1:12

Blessed is the one who perseveres under trial because, having stood the test, that person will receive the crown of life that the Lord has promised to those who love him.

WEEK 1, DAY 5

Chapter XXXIV

One of the monks, called Serapion, sold his book of the Gospels[5] and gave the money to those who were hungry, saying: I have sold the book which told me to sell all that I had and give to the poor.

Matthew 25:40

"The King will reply, 'Truly I tell you, whatever you did for one of the least of these brothers and sisters of mine, you did for me.'"

WEEK 1, DAY 6

Chapter XLIII

An elder said: Do not judge a fornicator if you are chaste, for if you do, you too are violating the law as much as he is. For He who said thou shalt not fornicate also said thou shalt not judge.

Matthew 6:14-15

"For if you forgive other people when they sin against you, your heavenly Father will also forgive you. But if you do not forgive others their sins, your Father will not forgive your sins."

---

5   Background note: It's important to note that in this particular time books were very costly, far more costly than in our day and age. Books were copied by hand which was one of the reasons for their high cost.

WEEK 1, DAY 7

APPLICATION QUESTIONS:

1. The monastic lifestyle can be a helpful reminder of the importance of building healthy spiritual rhythms into our daily life. Often in the gospels we read of Jesus withdrawing for private prayer or to be in solitude, practicing the presence of God. What spiritual rhythms are currently part of your daily life? How can you develop in this area and practice the presence God?

2. The monastics also help us focus on the Greatest Commandment: Loving God with all our heart, soul, mind and strength and loving our neighbor. How are you serving your neighbor? What practical thing can you do this week for one of your neighbors?

3. Occasionally the Church is accused of catering to the culture. Have you seen this to be true in your own context? If so, are there any steps you can take to remedy the situation? How can your current church learn from the Desert Father and Mothers?

ST. BENEDICT OF NURSIA

When it comes to Benedict, much of his life is "shrouded in ignorance and obscured by legend."[6] Most of what is known about him stems from the biography written about him by Gregory the Great. Benedict was born to a wealthy family, most likely around the year 480. He received his education in Rome, and while in the city he apparently was put off by the darkness and corruption he witnessed there. As a result, Benedict renounced his wealthy inheritance and sought solace in the Church of St. Peter Affili.[7]

This, however, would not be enough for Benedict. He apparently desired even greater solitude and withdrew to a cave in the area of Subiaco. During his three years in this location, Benedict earned a reputation as a holy and wise man. As word about him spread, he was eventually approached by some men who inquired of him to become the community's abbot.[8]

Supposedly, Benedict arrived and found the community of monks to be spiritually lazy and worldly. Benedict, himself a focused and obedient man, soon found the community did not favor his leadership and they attempted to poison him. He was spared, however, and returned to his life of solitude, pursuing God. In spite of this, he was approached by others who wanted him to lead their monastic community.[9] During this time Benedict wrote his Rule to guide monastic living, which still influences many believers to this day.

---

6   Woods, 87.
7   Ibid.
8   Ibid.
9   Ibid, 88.

It has been said that the root of St. Augustine's Rule was focused on love and the foundation of St. Benedict's Rule was built on obedience.[10] Benedict focused his monasteries on the core values of order, discipline, meekness, obedience, and humility, all organized around strict authority.[11] While this may not sit well with modern proclivities, this approach by Benedict fit the day and age in which God had placed this leader of the church.

This week's writings are taken from *The Rule of St. Benedict.*

WEEK 2, DAY 2

Prologue

Listen, O my son, to the precepts of thy master, and incline the ear of thy heart, and cheerfully receive and faithfully execute the admonitions of thy loving Father, that by the toil of obedience thou mayest return to Him from whom by sloth of disobedience thou hast gone away.

To thee, therefore, my speech is now directed, who giving up thine own will, takest up the strong and most excellent arms of obedience, to do battle for Christ the Lord, the true King.

Psalm 1:1-3

Blessed is the one who does not walk in step with the wicked or stand in the way that sinners take or sit in the company of mockers, but whose delight is in the law of the Lord, and who meditates on his law day and night. That person is like a tree planted by streams of water, which yields its fruit in season and whose leaf does not wither—whatever they do prospers.

---

10 Ibid, 86.
11 Ibid, 88.

Week 2, Day 2

Chapter II

When, therefore, anyone taketh the name of Abbot he should govern his disciples by a twofold teaching; namely, he should show them all that is good and holy by his deeds more than by his words; explain the commandments of God to intelligent disciples by words, but show the divine precepts to the dull and simple by his works.

James 3:1

Not many of you should become teachers, my fellow believers, because you know that we who teach will be judged more strictly.

Week 2, Day 3

Chapter V

The first degree of humility is obedience without delay….This obedience, however, will be acceptable to God and agreeable to men then only, if what is commanded is done without hesitation, delay, lukewarmness, grumbling or complaint, because the obedience which is rendered to Superior is rendered to God

Joshua 22:5

But be very careful to keep the commandment and the law that Moses the servant of the Lord gave you: to love the Lord your God, to walk in obedience to him, to keep his commands, to hold fast to him and to serve him with all your heart and with all your soul.

WEEK 2, DAY 4

Chapter VII

Let a man consider that God always seeth him from heaven, that the eye of God always beholdeth his works everywhere, and that the angels report them to Him every hour.

Psalm 139:7-10

Where can I go from your Spirit? Where can I flee from your presence? If I go up to the heavens, you are there; if I make my bed in the depths, you are there. If I rise on the wings of the dawn, if I settle on the far side of the sea, even there your hand will guide me, your right hand will hold me fast.

WEEK 2, DAY 5

Chapter XLVIII

Idleness is the enemy of the soul; and therefore the brethren ought to be employed in manual labor at certain times, at others, in devout reading.

2 Thessalonians 3:6-8

In the name of the Lord Jesus Christ, we command you, brothers and sisters, to keep away from every believer who is idle and disruptive and does not live according to the teaching[a] you received from us. For you yourselves know how you ought to follow our example. We were not idle when we were with you, nor did we eat anyone's food without paying for it. On the contrary, we worked night and day, laboring and toiling so that we would not be a burden to any of you.

Week 2, Day 6

Chapter LIII

Let all guests who arrive be received as Christ, because He will say: "I was a stranger and you took Me in" (Mt 25:35)…Let the greatest care be taken, especially in the reception of the poor and travelers, because Christ is received more specially in them; whereas regard for the wealthy itself procureth them respect.

James 2:1-6

My brothers and sisters, believers in our glorious Lord Jesus Christ must not show favoritism. Suppose a man comes into your meeting wearing a gold ring and fine clothes, and a poor man in filthy old clothes also comes in. If you show special attention to the man wearing fine clothes and say, "Here's a good seat for you," but say to the poor man, "You stand there" or "Sit on the floor by my feet," have you not discriminated among yourselves and become judges with evil thoughts? Listen, my dear brothers and sisters: Has not God chosen those who are poor in the eyes of the world to be rich in faith and to inherit the kingdom he promised those who love him? But you have dishonored the poor. Is it not the rich who are exploiting you? Are they not the ones who are dragging you into court?

WEEK 2, DAY 7

APPLICATION QUESTIONS:

1. Benedict brought a disciplined approach to his monasteries. Would you say that your approach to your faith-walk is a disciplined approach? Why or why not? What is an area of your walk that could benefit from more discipline?
2. How can a believer practice a disciplined faith without slipping into legalism? Have you ever dealt with legalism personally?
3. Discipline issues can often be sticky situations in the life of the church. How does your church deal with discipline? What can your church learn from Benedict's approach?

THE WAY OF A PILGRIM

The Way of a Pilgrim is a book that appears to be shrouded in some mystery. As Father Thomas Hopko mentions:

> The origin of this little spiritual classic is in many ways a mystery. No one knows for certain if it is a literally true story written by the narrator, or an account cast in the first person *about* a particular pilgrim (or perhaps based on several), or even a marvelously creative piece of spiritual fiction intended to propagate a certain understanding of the practice of the Orthodox Christian faith, and the prayer of the heart, particularly the Jesus Prayer.[12]

The focus of this work, believed to have been written sometime in the 19th century Russia, is the inner prayer of the heart, or the Jesus Prayer. This type of mysticism, which dates back much further than the 19th century, is also referred to as *Hesychasm*. The Jesus Prayer is the prayer found in the story of the Parable of the Pharisee and the Tax Collector in Luke 18:9-14. The Tax Collector prays: "God, have mercy on me, a sinner." The practice of *Hesychasm* involves the repetition of this pray, almost in a mantra-like, meditative state.

The story's main character, the pilgrim, is struck by the Apostle Paul's words in 1 Thessalonians 5:17: Pray without ceasing. As a result, the pilgrim sets out on a journey to learn the Jesus Prayer and seek solitude and a mystical connection with God. Along the way the pilgrim encounters a plethora of other people: some bringing blessings while others bring difficulty.

---

12 Olga Savin, trans. *The Way of a Pilgrim* and *The Pilgrim Continues His Way* (Shambhala Publications: Boston, 2001) pg. vii.

WEEK 3, DAY 2

Narrative 1, page 2

Unceasing interior prayer is the continual striving of man's spirit toward God. To succeed in this delightful exercise, you must beseech the Lord more frequently that He teach you how to pray unceasingly. Pray more and ever more earnestly, and the prayer itself will reveal to you how it can become unceasing. This effort will take its own time.

1 Thessalonians 5:17

Pray without ceasing.

WEEK 3, DAY 3

First Narrative, page 3

Those words of the apostle—'pray without ceasing'—should be understood in reference to the prayer of the mind: for the mind can always aspire to God and pray to Him without ceasing.

Isaiah 26:3

You will keep in perfect peace those whose minds are steadfast, because they trust in you.

WEEK 3, DAY 4

First Narrative, page 6

Many good works are required of a Christian, but it is prayer that must come first and foremost, for without prayer no other good work can be performed and one cannot find the way to the Lord.

John 15:5

"I am the vine; you are the branches. If you remain in me and I in you, you will bear much fruit; apart from me you can do nothing."

WEEK 3, DAY 5

Second Narrative, pages 17-18

[After the pilgrim's few belongings were stolen] "Let this be a lesson to you in detachment from earthly material possessions; it will ease your journey toward heaven. This was permitted to happen to you to protect you from falling into spiritual gluttony. God wants from the Christian a complete denial of his own will, of his desires and of all attachment to them, so that he can totally submit himself to His Divine Will."

Matthew 6:33

"But seek first his kingdom and his righteousness,…"

WEEK 3, DAY 6

Second Narrative, page 27

A person must acquire wisdom and strengthen himself as much as possible with the word of God against the spiritual enemy.

Ephesians 6:10-12

    Finally, be strong in the Lord and in his mighty power. Put on the full armor of God, so that you can take your stand against the devil's schemes. For our struggle is not against flesh and blood, but against the rulers, against the authorities, against the powers of this dark world and against the spiritual forces of evil in the heavenly realms.

WEEK 3, DAY 7

APPLICATION QUESTIONS:

1. In *The Way of a Pilgrim* the Pilgrim seems to focus on seeking a life of unceasing prayer based on Paul's words in 1 Thessalonians 5:17 ("Pray without ceasing"). Do you think it is possible for a Christ-follower to practice unceasing prayer? What do you think it would take for a Christian to pray without ceasing?
2. The Pilgrim practiced Hesychasm, also known as the Jesus Prayer. This involves seclusion and solitude while repeating the following prayer: "Lord Jesus Christ, have mercy on me, a sinner." Have you ever engaged in a practice such as this? Do you see any problems with a practice like this? Try it for a few days and journal any thoughts or occurrences that come to mind.
3. Is there any way for a practice such as Hesychasm to be applied to the Church-at-large, or is it something to be reserved more for private practice of the faith?

AELRED OF RIEVAULX

In the twelfth century the influence of Cistercian monasticism reached northward to England. This movement manifested in the building of Rievaulx Abbey in the area of Yorkshire.[13] A short time after the construction of Rievaulx, a young man from Scotland was sent on a mission to the Archbishop of York who was the patron of the abbey. This young man's name was Ethelred, who would later be known as Aelred (1110 – 1167). He petitioned the Abbey to be permitted to enter as a monk.[14]

Aelred would eventually rise to the position of abbot and under his solid leadership the Rievaulx Abbey would grow to become home to over six hundred Cistercian monks.[15] This was considered, in some ways, to be a golden era. There was relative peace during this time and it can be witnessed in Aelred's most popular writing, *On Spiritual Friendship*. On this work Dennis Billy writes:

> *On Friendship*, Aelred approaches his subject from a decidedly religious standpoint, examining both the theoretical and practical aspects of friendship in the light of faith in Christ. Christian friendship, he maintains, is all about extending the fellowship of Christ to another. The more two persons grow as friends, the more they should sense the gentle, unobtrusive, yet abiding presence of this quiet third partner in their lives.[16]

---

13 Woods, 130.
14 Ibid.
15 Ibid.
16 Aelred of Rievaulx, *Spiritual Friendship: The Classic Test with a Spiritual Commentary by Dennis Billy, C.Ss.R* (Notre Dame: Ave Maria Press, 2008) pg. 1.

This week's reading selections are taken from Aelred's *Spiritual Friendship*.

WEEK 4, DAY 2

Book 1, Section 8, 16

Therefore, these things which have already been said, even though they are in harmony with reason, and other things which the utility of this discussion demands that we treat, I should like proved to me with the authority of the Scriptures. I should like also to be instructed more fully as to how the friendship which ought to exist among us begins in Christ, is preserved according to the Spirit of Christ, and how its end and fruition are referred to in Christ....I confess that I am convinced that true friendship cannot exist among those who live without Christ.

1 Samuel 20:42

Jonathan said to David, "Go in peace, for we have sworn friendship with each other in the name of the Lord, saying, 'The Lord is witness between you and me, and between your descendants and my descendants forever.'"

WEEK 4, DAY 3

Book 1, Section 37-38

Let us allow that, because of some similarity in feelings, those friendships which are not true, be, nevertheless, called friendships, provided, however, they are judiciously distinguished from that friendship which is spiritual and therefore true. Hence let one kind of friendship be called carnal, another worldly, and another spiritual. The carnal springs from mutual harmony in vice; the worldly is enkindled by the hope of gain; and the spiritual is cemented by similarity of life, morals, and pursuits among the just.

Proverbs 12:26
The righteous choose their friends carefully, but the way of the wicked leads them astray.

WEEK 4, DAY 4

Book 1, Section 45

For spiritual friendship, which we call true, should be desired, not for consideration of any worldly advantage or for any extrinsic cause, but from the dignity of its own nature and the feelings of the human heart, so that its fruition and reward if nothing other than itself.

Proverbs 18:24

One who has unreliable friends soon comes to ruin, but there is a friend who sticks closer than a brother.

Week 4, Day 5

Book 1, Section 57

Finally, when God created man, in order to commend more highly the good of society, he said: "It is not good for man to be alone: let us make him a helper like unto himself." It was from no similar, nor even from the same, material that divine Might formed this help mate, but as a clearer inspiration to charity and friendship he produced the woman from the very substance of the man. How beautiful it is that the second human being was taken from the side of the first, so that nature might teach that human beings are equal and, as it were, collateral, and that there is in human affairs neither a superior nor an inferior, a characteristic of true friendship.

Ephesians 5:21; James 2:1

Submit to one another out of reverence for Christ.... My brothers and sisters, believers in our glorious Lord Jesus Christ must not show favoritism.

Week 4, Day 6

Book 2, Section 9, 12, 13

I do not presume that I can explain it in a manner benefiting the dignity of so signal a good, since in human affairs nothing more sacred is striven for, nothing more useful is sought after, nothing more difficult is discovered, nothing more sweet experienced, and nothing more profitable possessed. For friendship bears fruit in this life and in the next…"A friend," says the Wise Man, "is the medicine of life"… Friendship, therefore, heightens the joys of prosperity and mitigates the sorrows of adversity by dividing and sharing them. Hence, the best medicine in life is a friend.

Proverbs 27:17

As iron sharpens iron, so one person sharpens another.

WEEK 4, DAY 7

APPLICATION QUESTIONS:

1. Aelred believed that true friendship cannot be found between non-Christians. Do you agree with this viewpoint? Why or why not?
2. Aelred mentions that there are three types of friendships: carnal, worldly and spiritual. The carnal is built around vice, the worldly around personal gain, and the spiritual around Christ and the betterment of the other. Evaluate your friendships in light of these three categories. Are there any changes you feel you need to make as a result?
3. How do you think the local Church can apply the teachings of Aelred? Is this a topic the Church should focus on more often? Do you think may be important for discipleship and mentoring in the local Church? If so, how?

St. Bonaventure

Saint Bonaventure was born John of Fidanza (1217-74) and was born into a noble Italian family. Apparently, as a young child he was cured of a serious illness when his mother prayed to St. Francis of Assisi for help. In 1243 John would join the Franciscan Order of Paris, enter into the university and, as was custom, receive a new name—Bonaventure.[17]

Bonaventure had a remarkable career as a scholar. This led to him occupy the chair of theology at the University of Paris. In 1257 he was elected as Minister General of the Franciscan Order and he worked tirelessly to join together the feuding branches of his Order.[18] It was also during this time that he began to write his best-known works: *The Soul's Journey in to God*, *The Tree of Life* and *The Life of St. Francis*.

> Bonaventure's major spiritual work, *The Soul's Journey into God*, continues and develops Francis' mystical sense of God's presence in creation. Bonaventure saw the entire universe both as a mirror that reflected God and as a ladder of ascent by which we pass over into God. The powers of the human soul, similarly, both image God and also lead to union with God. His spirituality was, moreover, intensely Christ-centered, for Jesus was ultimately not only the ladder, but the door, the goal as well as the way.[19]

---

17 Woods, 149.
18 Ibid.
19 Ibid.

It's also worth noting that as a Franciscan, Bonaventure didn't merely live a contemplative life. They combined the contemplative life along with living in the world.

For our devotional purposes, we will utilize selections from *The Soul's Journey into God* and *The Tree of Life*.

WEEK 5, DAY 2

The Soul's Journey into God, Chapter 1, Section 8

Just as no one comes to wisdom except through grace, justice and knowledge, so no one comes to contemplation except by penetrating meditation, a holy life and devout prayer. Since grace is the foundation of the rectitude of the will and of the penetrating light of reason, we must first pray, then live holy lives and thirdly concentrate our attention upon the reflections of truth.

2 Corinthians 2:14-16

The person without the Spirit does not accept the things that come from the Spirit of God but considers them foolishness, and cannot understand them because they are discerned only through the Spirit. The person with the Spirit makes judgments about all things, but such a person is not subject to merely human judgments, for, "Who has known the mind of the Lord so as to instruct him?" But we have the mind of Christ.

WEEK 5, DAY 3

The Soul's Journey into God, Chapter 1, Section 15

Whoever, therefore, is not enlightened by such splendor of created things is blind; whoever is not awakened by such outcries is deaf; whoever does not praise God because of all these effects is dumb; whoever does not discover the First Principle from such clear signs is a fool. Therefore, open your eyes, alert the ears of your spirit, open your lips and apply your heart so that in all creatures you may see, hear, praise, love and worship, glorify and honor your God lest the whole world rise against you.

John 9:35-41

Jesus heard that they had thrown him out, and when he found him, he said, "Do you believe in the Son of Man?" "Who is he, sir?" the man asked. "Tell me so that I may believe in him." Jesus said, "You have now seen him; in fact, he is the one speaking with you." Then the man said, "Lord, I believe," and he worshiped him. Jesus said, "For judgment I have come into this world, so that the blind will see and those who see will become blind." Some Pharisees who were with him heard him say this and asked, "What? Are we blind too?" Jesus said, "If you were blind, you would not be guilty of sin; but now that you claim you can see, your guilt remains.

WEEK 5, DAY 4

The Soul's Journey into God, Chapter 3, Section 2, 3

In its first activity, therefore—the actual retention of all temporal things, past, present and future—the memory is an image of eternity, whose indivisible presence extends to all times....From this it is obvious that our intellect is joined to Eternal Truth itself since it can grasp no truth with certitude if it is not taught by this Truth.

Ecclesiastes 3:11

He has made everything beautiful in its time. He has also set eternity in the human heart; yet no one can fathom what God has done from beginning to end.

WEEK 5, DAY 5

The Soul's Journey into God, Chapter Four, Section 1

When one has fallen down, he must lie there unless someone lend a helping hand for him to rise. So our soul could not rise completely from these things of sense to see itself and the Eternal Truth in itself unless Truth, assuming human nature in Christ, had become a ladder, restoring the first ladder that had been broken in Adam.

John 1:50-51

Jesus said, "You believe because I told you I saw you under the fig tree. You will see greater things than that." He then added, "Very truly I tell you, you will see 'heaven open, and the angels of God ascending and descending on' the Son of Man."

WEEK 5, DAY 6

The Tree of Life, Prologue, Section 3

Picture in your mind a tree whose roots are watered by an ever-flowing fountain that becomes a great and living river with four channels to water the garden of the entire Church. From the trunk of this tree, imagine that there are growing twelve branches that are adorned with leaves, flowers and fruit....This fruit is offered to God's servants to be tested so that when they eat it, they may always be satisfied, yet never grow weary of its taste.

Revelation 22:1-3

Then the angel showed me the river of the water of life, as clear as crystal, flowing from the throne of God and of the Lamb down the middle of the great street of the city. On each side of the river stood the tree of life, bearing twelve crops of fruit, yielding its fruit every month. And the leaves of the tree are for the healing of the nations. No longer will there be any curse. The throne of God and of the Lamb will be in the city, and his servants will serve him.

WEEK 5, DAY 7

APPLICATION QUESTIONS:

1. Bonaventure mentions the importance of being illuminated by God. Since coming to faith in Jesus Christ, how has God opened your eyes? What are some things that you see and understand differently today as a result?
2. What do you think it means that God has placed "eternity in the heart of humanity" (Eccl. 3:11)? Have you seen this to be true in your own life and experience?
3. What are some ways in which the local Church can apply the importance of illumination? Do you see any possible dangers with this?

Thomas a Kempis
1380 – 1471

THOMAS A KEMPIS

Thomas a Kempis (1380-1471) was born Thomas Hemerken in the area of Kempen, Germany. He was educated in Deventer under the Brethren of the Common Life. Thomas received his habit of a Canon Regular in 1406 at the age of twenty-six.[20] His most successful writing was *The Imitation of Christ*. This work is one of the most widely read devotionals still to this day.

Thomas' writing falls into what could be called *devotio moderna*, or "modern devotion."[21] "This 'modern devotion' was rooted in the heart rather than the head, extolled feeling over thought, and tended to view the world negatively as a whole."[22] This style of writing was drastically different from the mystics who had come before Thomas. Their approach tended to be more radical and focus mostly on the head as opposed to the senses or the heart.

The time of Thomas' writing must also be taken into account. He wrote in the fifteenth century which was both a time when the church was flourishing in some areas, but it was also what some refer to as "the autumn of Christendom."[23] Only about fifty years after Thomas a Kempis would Martin Luther nail his 95 Theses on the door of Wittenberg Church and forever change the religious landscape of Europe.

The effects of this can be seen on Thomas' writing. Often he comes across as bleak, other-worldly and anti-intellectual.[24] Thom-

---

20 Woods, 172.
21 Ibid.
22 Ibid.
23 Ibid.
24 Ibid.

as a Kempis spent the majority of his life cloistered away in solitude, avoiding the bleak world around him.

Our selected readings are taken from his longstanding work, *The Imitation of Christ.*

WEEK 6, DAY 2

Book 1, Chapter III, Section 5

Of a surety, at the Day of Judgment it will be demanded of us, not what we have read, but what we have done; not how well we have spoken, but how holily we have lived.

James 2:14-17

What good is it, my brothers and sisters, if someone claims to have faith but has no deeds? Can such faith save them? Suppose a brother or a sister is without clothes and daily food. If one of you says to them, "Go in peace; keep warm and well fed," but does nothing about their physical needs, what good is it? In the same way, faith by itself, if it is not accompanied by action, is dead.

WEEK 6, DAY 3

Book 1, Chapter VII, Section 1

Vain is the life of that man that putteth his trust in men or in any created Thing. Be not ashamed to be the servant of others for the love of Jesus Christ, and be reckoned poor in this life.

Luke 22:25-27

Jesus said to them, "The kings of the Gentiles lord it over them; and those who exercise authority over them call themselves Benefactors. But you are not to be like that. Instead, the greatest among you should be like the youngest, and the one who rules like the one who serves. For who is greater, the one who is at the table or the one who serves? Is it not the one who is at the table? But I am among you as one who serves.

WEEK 6, DAY 4

Book 1, Chapter XI, Section 5

If each year should see one fault rooted out from us, we should go quickly on to perfection. But on the contrary, we often feel that we are better and holier in the beginning of our conversion than after many years of profession. Zeal and progress ought to increase day by day; yet now it seemeth a great thing if one is able to retain some portion of his first ardour.

Revelation 2:4-5a

"Yet I hold this against you: You have forsaken the love you had at first. Consider how far you have fallen! Repent and do the things you did at first."

WEEK 6, DAY 5

Book 1, Chapter XIX, Section 4

Gird up thy loins like a man against the assaults of the devil; bridle thine appetite, and thou wilt soon be able to bridle every inclination of the flesh. Be thou never without something to do; be reading, or writing, or praying, or meditating, or doing something that is useful to the community.

2 Thessalonians 3:11-13

We hear that some among you are idle and disruptive. They are not busy; they are busybodies. Such people we command and urge in the Lord Jesus Christ to settle down and earn the food they eat. And as for you, brothers and sisters, never tire of doing what is good.

WEEK 6, DAY 6

Book 2, Chapter II, Section 1

Make no great account who is for thee or who is against thee, but mind only the present duty and take care that God be with thee in whatsoever thou doest. Have a good conscience and God will defend thee, for he whom God will help no man's perverseness shall be able to hurt. If thou knowest how to hold thy peace and to suffer, without doubt thou shalt see the help of the Lord.

2 Corinthians 1:12

Now this is our boast: Our conscience testifies that we have conducted ourselves in the world, and especially in our relations with you, with integrity and godly sincerity. We have done so, relying not on worldly wisdom but on God's grace.

WEEK 6, DAY 7

APPLICATION QUESTIONS:

1. Thomas a Kempis seemed to focus on the practical side of the faith stemming from the heart. How do you strive to balance the contemplative/meditative side of the faith and the obedient/practical side? Do you favor one side over the other? What do you need to do about that?

2. Do you examine your faith-walk often? How do you measure spiritual growth in your walk with Jesus Christ?

3. What are some ways in which the Church can encourage others to find a balanced approach to their faith-walk? What does your current Church utilize? Is there a way to measure the spiritual health of a local Church?

JULIAN OF NORWICH

Julian of Norwich (c.1342 – c.1416) is an historical figure shrouded in mystery. No one knows who she truly was. She has "evaded every attempt to uncover her identity."[25] Her name comes from the church in Norwich, England. It was here that she was walled into a solitary cell where "she would spend the rest of her life in prayer and contemplation."[26]

While her true identity remains a mystery, we do know some key points about Julian's life. For instance, on May 8, 1373, Julian became extremely ill with a disease, possibly the Plague, which brought her near death. During this time she received fifteen visions "during an ecstasy that lasted about five hours."[27] When this finished she found herself cured from the disease. That next day Julian received another vision that supposedly clarified the previous fifteen.

Her most well-known writing is *Showings of Divine Love*. This is essentially an account of the visions she received while suffering from disease. For Julian, the emphasis on one's spiritual journey and thus the emphasis of her work revolve around the love of God. "God as pure love is the origin, the goal, the way, the means, and the motive of everything that is."[28] Julian wrote at a time of great turmoil and fear due in large part to the effects of the Plague. A theme that resounds through her work is the optimistic message that God can bring good out the evil in the world.[29]

---

25 Ibid, 165.
26 Ibid.
27 Ibid.
28 Ibid.
29 Ibid.

For our devotional, we have selected passages from the Long Text of *Showings of Divine Love.*

WEEK 7, DAY 2

The Long Text, Chapter 21

I understood that we are now, as our Lord intends it, dying with him on his cross in our pain and our passion; and if we willingly remain on the same cross with his help and his grace until the final moment, the countenance he turns on us will suddenly change, and we shall be with him in heaven.

Matthew 16:24-25

Then Jesus said to his disciples, "Whoever wants to be my disciple must deny themselves and take up their cross and follow me. For whoever wants to save their life will lose it, but whoever loses their life for me will find it."

WEEK 7, DAY 3

The Long Text, Chapter 43

Prayer unites the soul to God; for though the soul, restored through grace, is always like God in nature and substance, yet because of sin on man's part, it is often in a state which is unlike God. Then prayer testifies that the desire of the soul is the desire of God, and it comforts the conscience and fits man to receive grace.

1 Peter 5:6-8

Humble yourselves, therefore, under God's mighty hand, that he may lift you up in due time. Cast all your anxiety on him because he cares for you. Be alert and of sober mind. Your enemy the devil prowls around like a roaring lion looking for someone to devour.

WEEK 7, DAY 4

The Long Text, Chapter 51

And then I saw that only suffering blames and punishes, and our kind Lord comforts and grieves; he always considers the soul cheerfully, loving and longing to bring us to bliss.

Matthew 5:4

"Blessed are those who mourn, for they will be comforted."

WEEK 7, DAY 5

The Long Text, Chapter 56

God wants this to begin here in the knowledge of his love; for we cannot profit from our reason alone, unless we also have perception and love; nor can we be saved just because we are naturally grounded in God, unless we have knowledge of this ground and of his mercy and grace, for from these three, working all together, we receive all our goodness.

1 Corinthians 13:1-3

If I speak in the tongues of men or of angels, but do not have love, I am only a resounding gong or a clanging cymbal. If I have the gift of prophecy and can fathom all mysteries and all knowledge, and if I have a faith that can move mountains, but do not have love, I am nothing. If I give all I possess to the poor and give over my body to hardship that I may boast, but do not have love, I gain nothing.

WEEK 7, DAY 6

The Long Text, Chapter 64

It is more blessed for man to be taken from suffering than for suffering to be taken from man; for if pain is taken from us it may return. Therefore it is a supreme comfort and blessed insight for a loving soul that we shall be taken from pain; for in this promise I saw the marvelous compassion which our Lord has for us in our woe and his kind promise of complete deliverance.

Philippians 3:10-11

I want to know Christ—yes, to know the power of his resurrection and participation in his sufferings, becoming like him in his death, and so, somehow, attaining to the resurrection from the dead.

WEEK 7, DAY 7

APPLICATION QUESTIONS:

1. In our selected readings Julian of Norwich seems to speak often of suffering. Have you experienced suffering in your life? What was the effect of that suffering? Did it draw you closer to God?
2. Julian mentions that a believer must die "with him on his cross in our pain and our passion" (see Week 7, Day 2). What, if anything, did you have to part with when you submitted to the lordship of Jesus Christ? Is there anything God may be calling you to lay aside currently?
3. How has your current Church dealt with the issues of suffering and sacrifice for the sake of the cross? Is there anything you would change about their approach, view, etc.?

MARTIN LUTHER (1483 – 1546)

The sixteenth century found the Church falling on tumultuous times. "Already sundered from the Eastern (Orthodox) Church for almost five hundred years," writes Woods, "in the sixteenth century the Western (Catholic) branch began to ramify prolifically. Lutheran, Anabaptist, Reformed and Calvinist, Anglican, Puritan, Quaker, Methodist and Baptist churches represent only the principal European offshoots."[30] This time period is often referred to as the Protestant Reformation.

Regarding the Reformation, the most prominent name is that of Martin Luther. This is due in large part to Luther's nailing of the Ninety-five Theses to the door of the church in Wittenburg in 1517. While ultimately beginning the Protestant Reformation, Luther himself never intended to break away from the Catholic branch of the church. Rather, he desired to reform the church from the inside out. Particularly, Luther wanted the church to deal with the issue of the selling of indulgences and re-evaluate its stance on works-based righteousness.

Luther, the son of a miner, was born in Eisleben, Germany in 1483.[31] After entering into the monastery of the Augustine Hermits and his Ordination in 1507, he was sent to Rome. While in Rome he was "scandalized" by the crude behavior he witnessed.[32] After returning from Rome he was sent to teach at the University of Wittenburg. It was while teaching here that Luther experienced his "breakthrough" in regard to the issue of justification. Luther

---

30   Ibid, 185.
31   Ibid, 186.
32   Ibid.

came to understand that "God's grace alone justifies the human soul through faith, and, as St. Paul and St. Augustine had insisted, good works do not 'earn' God's favor but demonstrate it."[33] This would have a profound effect on the Church and history as we know it today.

Our reading selections this week are taken from Martin Luther's booklet, *A Simple Way to Pray*. Luther wrote this in 1535 for a friend and barber, Peter Beskendorf, in response to his friend's inquiries regarding a life of prayer. Throughout this booklet it is obvious that for Luther, prayer is directly related to time spent with the Word of God.[34]

WEEK 8, DAY 2

Page 3

It is a good thing to let prayer be the first business of the morning and the last at night. Guard yourself carefully against those false, deluding ideas which tell you, "Wait a little while. I will pray in an hour; first I must attend to this or that." Such thoughts get you away from prayer into other affairs which so hold your attention and involve you that nothing comes of prayer for that day.

Mark 1:35

Very early in the morning, while it was still dark, Jesus got up, left the house and went off to a solitary place, where he prayed.

---

33 Ibid, 187.
34 Martin Luther, "A Simple Way to Pray." In *Luther's Works*, Vol. 43, Page 193-211.

WEEK 8, DAY 3

Page 7

Finally, mark this, that you must always speak the Amen firmly. Never doubt that God in his mercy will surely hear you and say "yes" to your prayers….Do not leave your prayer without having said or thought, "Very well, God has heard my prayer; this I know as certainty and a truth." That is what Amen means.

Psalm 5:2-3

Hear my cry for help, my King and my God, for to you I pray. In the morning, Lord, you hear my voice; in the morning I lay my requests before you and wait expectantly.

WEEK 8, DAY 4

Page 9

[When praying through the Ten Commandments] I think of each commandment as, first, instruction, which is really what it is intended to be, and consider what the Lord God demands of me so earnestly. Second, I turn it into a thanksgiving; third, a confession; and fourth, a prayer.

Philippians 4:6-7

Do not be anxious about anything, but in every situation, by prayer and petition, with thanksgiving, present your requests to God. And the peace of God, which transcends all understanding, will guard your hearts and your minds in Christ Jesus.

WEEK 8, DAY 5

Page 3

First, when I feel that I have become cool and joyless in prayer because of other tasks or thoughts (for the flesh and the devil always impede and obstruct our prayer), I take my little psalter, hurry to my room, or, if it be that day and hour for it, to the church where a congregation is assembled and, as time permits, I say quietly to myself and word-for-word the Ten Commandments, the Creed, and, if I have time, some words of Christ or of Paul, or some psalms, just as a child might do.

Psalm 119:105

Your word is a lamp for my feet, a light on my path.

WEEK 8, DAY 6

Page 16

In addition I give thanks for his steadfast goodness in that he has given such excellent teachings, assurance, and protection to me and to all the world. If it were not for his protection, not a penny or a crumb of bread would be left in the house....We owe him thanks both for his teachings and the protection which he has graciously provided for us.

1 Thessalonians 5:16-18

Rejoice always, pray continually, give thanks in all circumstances; for this is God's will for you in Christ Jesus.

WEEK 8, DAY 7

APPLICATION QUESTIONS:

1. What do I do when I find myself in a "dry time" of prayer? Do I pray Scripture as Martin Luther suggests?[35]
2. How often do I pray prayers of thanksgiving to God? Do I need to do it more?
3. Do I practice prayer at regular times of day, such as the morning and evening as Martin Luther suggests? If not, how can I start to schedule my prayer time more diligently this week?

---

35 Check out the appendix for other methods of prayer: Ignatian prayer and Lectio Divina.

ST. JOHN OF THE CROSS (1542 – 1591)

John of the Cross was born in Spain to Gonzalo Yepes and Catalina Alvarez in the year 1542. His father was from a wealthy family who made their way in the silk trade while his mother was a poor weaver. Their marriage was opposed by Gonzalo's wealthy family, ultimately resulting in his family disowning him.[36] John, who was the youngest of three boys, was raised in poverty.

John's life was one that seemed to be marked with tragedy, loss, and even betrayal. At a very young age, his father died which left the family in a dire situation. His mother sought help from her late husband's family only to find rejection. Catalina eventually found assistance through a school for the poor that would provide education and some food for her family.

During this time period the Plague was a major issue in Europe. This was one set of recurring pandemics, starting with the Black Death in the 14th century. These recurrences of the plague were frequently linked with resurgences of spiritual renewal. Perhaps this is part of John's story. At the age of seventeen John went to work in the local Plague hospital in Medina del Campo.[37] This experience would lead to more death and darkness in his life. But there was also some good news because it was here that John was also admitted into the local Jesuit College. From the years 1559 to 1563 John received a classic education. Also, during this time his patron, Don Alonso Alvarez, supported John's theological studies with the intention that he would work as a chaplain at the Plague

---

36 Woods, 208.
37 Ibid, 209.

hospital.[38] During this time John was drawn to the Carmelite Order and he entered the Order in 1563. From here John would go on to the college at Salamanca. As a result of his outstanding abilities, John was named Prefect of Studies for the Carmelites and in 1567 he was ordained.[39] A short time later John was considering a switch to the Carthusian Order, until he met with St. Teresa of Avila who would help him change his mind. Teresa also sought John's help in reforming the whole Carmelite Order. John agreed, but this would bring more hardship into his life.

Misunderstanding between the two branches of the Carmelite Order (the Calced[40] and the Discalced[41], or reformed) led to John eventually being imprisoned by the Calced Carmelites. For nearly one year John was held in a dark, tiny cell and he was scourged repeatedly by his captors. John, however, did manage to escape and find refuge at a convent of Discalced nuns in Toledo.[42] Later on, John was even banished and his enemies sought to have him expelled from the Order.[43]

Even at the end of his life it seems John had to wrestle with difficulty. Due to his ailing health he was sent to Ubeda for treatment. While there he was assigned the worst cell and was treated harshly. Regularly he was reminded of being a burden to his caregivers as well as the high cost of his treatment.[44] Humble to the end, however, on his death bed John asked for forgiveness for being burden and died in relative obscurity, which he actually desired.

John's writings have been very influential over the years. Some of his writings include *The Dark Night of the Soul*, which was inspired by his imprisonment, as well as *the living Flame of Love* and

---

38 Ibid.
39 Ibid.
40 Literally, those who wore shoes/footwear.
41 Literally, those who did not wear shoes/footwear. This was part of the medicant ("beggar") aesthetic associated with some of the monastic orders.
42 Woods,211.
43 Ibid.
44 Ibid.

The Ascent of Mount Carmel. For this devotional we have selected passages from *The Dark Night of the Soul* and *The Living Flame of Love*.

WEEK 9, DAY 2

The Dark Night, Chapter 2, Section 6

Souls, however, who are advancing in perfection act in an entirely different manner and with a different quality of spirit during this period. They receive great benefit from their humility by which they not only place little importance on their deeds, but also take very little self-satisfaction from them. They think everyone else is far better than themselves, and usually possess a holy envy of them and would like to emulate their service to God.

Romans 12:3

For by the grace given me I say to every one of you: Do not think of yourself more highly than you ought, but rather think of yourself with sober judgment, in accordance with the faith God has distributed to each of you.

WEEK 9, DAY 3

The Dark Night, Chapter 3, Section 2

They, therefore, who are well guided from the outset do not become attached to visible instruments or burden themselves with them. They do not care to know any more than what is necessary to accomplish good works, because their eyes are fixed only on God, on being His friend, and pleasing Him; this is what they long for.

Hebrews 12:1-2

Therefore, since we are surrounded by such a great cloud of witnesses, let us throw off everything that hinders and the sin that so easily entangles. And let us run with perseverance the race marked out for us, fixing our eyes on Jesus, the pioneer and perfecter of faith. For the joy set before him he endured the cross, scorning its shame, and sat down at the right hand of the throne of God.

WEEK 9, DAY 4

The Dark Night, Chapter 9, Section 3

There is, consequently, a notable difference between dryness and lukewarmness. The lukewarm are very lax and remiss in their will and spirit, and have no solicitude about serving God. Those suffering from the purgative dryness are ordinarily solicitous, concerned, and pained about not serving God. Even though this dryness may be furthered by melancholia or some other humor—as it often is—it does not thereby fail to produce its purgative effect in the appetite, for the soul will be deprived of every satisfaction and concerned only about God.

Revelation 3:15-16

I know your deeds, that you are neither cold nor hot. I wish you were either one or the other! So, because you are lukewarm—neither hot nor cold—I am about to spit you out of my mouth.

Week 9, Day 5

The Living Flame, Stanza 1, Section 3

The flame of love is the Spirit of its bridegroom, which is the Holy Spirit….Such is the activity of the Holy Spirit in the soul transformed in love: The interior acts He produces shoot up flames, for they are acts of inflamed love in which the will of the soul united with that flame, made one with it loves most sublimely.

Galatians 5:22-25

But the fruit of the Spirit is love, joy, peace, forbearance, kindness, goodness, faithfulness, gentleness and self-control. Against such things there is no law. Those who belong to Christ Jesus have crucified the flesh with its passions and desires. Since we live by the Spirit, let us keep in step with the Spirit.

Week 9, Day 6

The Living Flame, Stanza 4, Section 15

Oh, how happy is this soul that ever experiences God resting and reposing within it! Oh, how fitting it is for it to withdraw from things, flee from business matters, and live in immense tranquility, so that it may not even with the slightest mote or noise disturb or trouble its heart where the beloved dwells.

John 14:16-17

And I will ask the Father, and he will give you another advocate to help you and be with you forever—the

Spirit of truth. The world cannot accept him, because it neither sees him nor knows him. But you know him, for he lives with you and will be in you.

WEEK 9, DAY 7

APPLICATION QUESTIONS:

1. Have you ever experienced "dry times" in your walk with Jesus Christ? How did you get through them? Did anything change as a result?
2. What do you think are the differences between "dry times" and "the Dark Night of the Soul"?
3. How can the local Church body support those who are enduring through the Dark Night?

BROTHER LAWRENCE (C.1614 – 1691)[45]

In some ways, Brother Lawrence is one of those enigmatic figures from Church History much like that of Julian of Norwich. Brother Lawrence was born in France as Nicholas Herman. He did not have much education and he served briefly as a footman and a soldier. During his stint as a soldier in the 30 Years War he received an injury that affected his sciatic nerve. This would leave him crippled and in chronic pain the remainder of his life.

Before joining the army, however, Brother Lawrence experienced what could be called his conversion moment. Apparently, during one winter he was observing a leafless tree against the winter sky and he was struck by God's providence. Lawrence imagined himself as the tree waiting for God to bring it to life once again. This experience eventually led him to become a lay brother among the Discalced Carmelites in Paris in 1666. He was considered a lay brother due to his lack of education. It was from this point that Nicholas Herman would forever be known as "Brother Lawrence."

Brother Lawrence spent the majority of his time working in the monastery kitchen and also some time in a sandal repair shop. The deep spirituality of this humble lay brother lies in the focus on "the presence of God." Brother Lawrence had a way of making the most menial of tasks into an act of worship. This can be seen in a short prayer attributed to him:

Lord of all pots and pans and things…

---

45 Information for Brother Lawrence taken from: Brother Lawrence, *The Practice of the Presence of God with Spiritual Maxims* (Spire Books: Grand Rapids, 1967) pgs. 11-14; and class notes, Evangelical Seminary, Myerstown, PA, Summer 2013.

Make me a saint by getting meals
And washing up the plates!

Our selections for this week's devotions are extracted from Brother Lawrence's work *The Practice of the Presence of God.*

WEEK 10, DAY 2

Second Conversation

I engaged in a religious life only for the love of God, and I have endeavored to act only for Him; whatever becomes of me, whether I be lost or saved, I will always continue to act purely for the love of God. I shall have this good at least, that till death I shall have done all that is in me to love Him.

John 13:14-15; 34-35

Now that I, your Lord and Teacher, have washed your feet, you also should wash one another's feet. I have set you an example that you should do as I have done for you....A new command I give you: Love one another. As I have loved you, so you must love one another. By this everyone will know that you are my disciples, if you love one another.

WEEK 10, DAY 3

Second Conversation

That all bodily mortifications and other exercises are useless, except as they serve to arrive at the union with God by love; that he had well considered this, and found it the shortest way to go straight to Him by a continual exercise of love and doing all things for His sake. That we ought to make a great difference between the acts of the understanding and those of the will; that the first were comparatively of little value, and the other, all. That our only business was to love and delight ourselves sin God.

Deuteronomy 6:4-5

Hear, O Israel: The Lord our God, the Lord is one. Love the Lord your God with all your heart and with all your soul and with all your strength.

Week 10, Day 4

Third Conversation

That many do not advance in the Christian progress because they stick in penances and particular exercises, while they neglect the love of God, which is the *end*. That this appeared plainly by their works, and was the reason why we see so little solid virtue.

Matthew 23:23

Woe to you, teachers of the law and Pharisees, you hypocrites! You give a tenth of your spices—mint, dill and cumin. But you have neglected the more important matters of the law—justice, mercy and faithfulness. You should have practiced the latter, without neglecting the former.

WEEK 10, DAY 5

Fourth Conversation

That we might accustom ourselves to a continual conversation with Him, with freedom and in simplicity. That we need only to recognize God intimately present with us, to address ourselves to Him every moment, that we may beg His assistance for knowing His will in things doubtful, and for rightly performing which we plainly see He requires of us, offering them to Him before we do them, and giving thanks when we have done.

Psalm 139:7-12

Where can I go from your Spirit? Where can I flee from your presence? If I go up to the heavens, you are there; if I make my bed in the depths, you are there. If I rise on the wings of the dawn, if I settle on the far side of the sea, even there your hand will guide me, your right hand will hold me fast. If I say, "Surely the darkness will hide me and the light become night around me," even the darkness will not be dark to you; the night will shine like the day, for darkness is as light to you.

WEEK 10, DAY 6

Eleventh Letter

I do not pray that you may be delivered from your pains, but I pray God earnestly that He would give you strength and patience to bear them as long as He pleases. Comfort yourself with Him who holds you fastened to the cross. He will loose you when He thinks fit. Happy those who suffer with Him. Accustom yourself to suffer in that manner, and seek from Him the strength to endure as much, and as long, as He shall judge necessary for you. The men of the world do not comprehend these truths, nor is it to be wondered at, since they suffer like what they are, and not like Christians. They consider sickness as a pain to nature, and not as a favor from God; and seeing it only in that light, they find nothing in it but grief and distress. But those that consider sickness as coming from the hand of God, as the effect of His mercy, and the means which He employs for their salvation—such commonly find in it great sweetness and sensible consolation.

2 Corinthians 12:1-10

I must go on boasting. Although there is nothing to be gained, I will go on to visions and revelations from the Lord. I know a man in Christ who fourteen years ago was caught up to the third heaven. Whether it was in the body or out of the body I do not know—God knows. And I know that this man—whether in the body or apart from the body I do not know, but God knows—was caught up to paradise and heard inexpressible things, things that no one is permitted to tell. I will boast about a man like that, but I will not boast about myself, except about my weaknesses. Even if I should choose to boast, I would not be a fool, because I would be speaking the truth. But I refrain, so no one will think more of me than is warranted by what I do or say, or because of these surpassingly great revelations. Therefore, in order to keep me from becoming conceited, I was given a thorn in my flesh, a messenger of Satan, to torment me. Three times I pleaded with the Lord to take it away from me. But he said to me, "My grace is sufficient for you, for my power is made perfect in weakness." Therefore I will boast all the more gladly about my weaknesses, so that Christ's power may rest on me. That is why, for Christ's sake, I delight in weaknesses, in insults, in hardships, in persecutions, in difficulties. For when I am weak, then I am strong.

WEEK 10, DAY 7

APPLICATION QUESTIONS:

1. Do you ever stop to realize that God is with you at all times? How does this thought make you feel? Is there anything you would like to change about your daily living in light of this truth?
2. Brother Lawrence practices the presence of God while doing dishes and other "menial" tasks. What "menial" task do you regularly do and how can you imitate Brother Lawrence and practice the presence of God?
3. What ways does your local Church body practice the presence of God? Is this an area that could be improved upon for your Church? If so, how?

JOHN WESLEY (1703 – 1791)

John Wesley was born the fifteenth child to Samuel and Susanna Wesley in 1703 in Epworth, England. Wesley's upbringing was very strict in nature, and this would have an effect upon his life to come and especially upon his future ministry. His mother, Susanna, believed in the following principles of parenting: (1) spare the rod, spoil the child; (2) the root of all sin is self-will; and (3) sinful actions should be punished.

Wesley was ordained an Anglican priest in 1725 the following year he was offered a fellowship at Lincoln College, Oxford.[46] It was here that Wesley began to develop his "methodical" approach to spirituality. A number of years later, in 1736, John along with his brother, Charles, would sail for the American colonies, Georgia specifically, on a missionary venture. However, after failing miserably, John returned home to England to regroup. A short time later, in 1738, Wesley had what can be referred to as his "Aldersgate experience." While attending a Moravian meeting he heard someone reading the preface to Martin Luther's commentary on Romans and he suddenly felt his heart "strangely warmed." This would wind up being a major turning point for Wesley.

Wesley's methodical approach matched with his zeal would have spiritual impact not only upon Europe but also in America as well. As Richard Woods shares, "Often at odds with the Established Church, Wesley turned increasingly to the people themselves. Beginning in 1742, he traveled tirelessly on horseback throughout Britain, Scotland, Wales, and Ireland preaching and establishing centers of evangelism. In 1768, Methodism reached New York,

---

46 Woods, 228.

and in 1771 Wesley sent Francis Asbury to supervise the evangelical movement in America."[47]

Wesley stayed within the Anglican Church and, much like Martin Luther, had no desire to splinter off from the Church. However, there was eventually a break and Methodism became its own denomination within the Church.

Wesley is arguably most known for his teachings on prevenient grace and Christian perfection. He was forced to defend both of these doctrines quite often during his day. Our selected readings for this week are extracted from Wesley's work *A Plain Account of Christian Perfection*.

WEEK 11, DAY 2

Chapter 6

In the same sermon I observed, "'Love is the fulfillment of the law, the end of the commandment,' It is not only 'the first and great' command, but all the commandments, in one. 'Whatsoever things are just, whatsoever things are pure, if there be any virtue, if there be any praise,' they are all comprised in this one word, love. In this is perfection, and glory and happiness: the royal law of heaven and earth is this, "Thou shalt love the Lord thy God with all thy heart, and with all thy soul, and with all thy mind, and with all thy strength.' The one perfect good shall be your ultimate end.

James 2:8

If you really keep the royal law found in Scripture, "Love your neighbor as yourself," you are doing right.

---

47 Ibid.

WEEK 11, DAY 3

Chapter 13

This great gift of God, the salvation of our souls, is no other than the image of God fresh stamped on our hearts. It is a 'renewal of believers in the spirit of their minds, after the likeness of Him that created them.' God hath now laid 'the axe unto the root of the tree, purifying their hearts by faith,' and 'cleansing all the thoughts of their hearts by the inspiration of His Holy Spirit.' Having this hope, that they shall see God as He is, 'purify themselves even as He is pure,' and are 'holy, as He that hath called them is holy, in all manner of conversation.' Not that they have already attained all that they shall attain, either are already in this sense perfect. But they daily 'go on from strength to strength, beholding' now, 'as in a glass, the glory of the Lord, they are changed into the same image, from glory to glory, by the Spirit of the Lord.'

Colossians 3:5-10

Put to death, therefore, whatever belongs to your earthly nature: sexual immorality, impurity, lust, evil desires and greed, which is idolatry. Because of these, the wrath of God is coming. You used to walk in these ways, in the life you once lived. But now you must also rid yourselves of all such things as these: anger, rage, malice, slander, and filthy language from your lips. Do not lie to each other, since you have taken off your old self with its practices and have put on the new self, which is being renewed in knowledge in the image of its Creator.

WEEK 11, DAY 4

Chapter 19

"What is Christian perfection?"

"The loving God with all our heart, mind, soul, and strength. This implies, that no wrong temper, none contrary to love, remains in the soul; and that all the thoughts, words and actions, are governed by pure love."

1 John 4:16b-21

God is love. Whoever lives in love lives in God, and God in them. This is how love is made complete among us so that we will have confidence on the day of judgment: In this world we are like Jesus. There is no fear in love. But perfect love drives out fear, because fear has to do with punishment. The one who fears is not made perfect in love. We love because he first loved us. Whoever claims to love God yet hates a brother or sister is a liar. For whoever does not love their brother and sister, whom they have seen, cannot love God, whom they have not seen. And he has given us this command: Anyone who loves God must also love their brother and sister.

WEEK 11, DAY 5

Chapter 25, Section 32

Watch and pray continually against pride. If God has cast it out, see that it enter no more; it is full as dangerous as desire. And you may slide back into it unawares; especially if you think there is no danger of it....Let modesty and self-diffidence appear in all your words and actions.

Let all you speak and do show that you are little, and base, and mean, and vile in your own eyes.

1 Peter 5:5b-6

All of you, clothe yourselves with humility toward one another, because, "God opposes the proud but shows favor to the humble." Humble yourselves, therefore, under God's mighty hand, that he may lift you up in due time.

Week 11, Day 6

Chapter 25, Section 38

Be exemplary in all things; particularly in outward things (as in dress), in little things, in the laying out of your money (avoiding every needless expense), in deep, steady seriousness, and in solidity and usefulness of all your conversation....Humility and patience are the surest proofs of the increase of love....True humility is a kind of self-annihilation, and this is the center of all virtues.

Titus 2:7-8

In everything set them an example by doing what is good. In your teaching show integrity, seriousness and soundness of speech that cannot be condemned, so that those who oppose you may be ashamed because they have nothing bad to say about us.

Week 11, Day 7

Application Questions:

1. For Wesley, Christian perfection does not entail sinlessness but rather loving God wholeheartedly. Do you agree with Wesley? Do you think it is possible for a Christian to reach perfection before glorification?

2. Love, both God's love for humanity and humanity's love for God, was a very important concept for Wesley. How has God's love impacted your life? Have you ever struggled to receive God's love? How are you showing your love for God in your own context?

3. How is your local Church demonstrating the love of God and humility within its own neighborhood? If your Church disappeared, would the community notice?

THOMAS KELLY (1893 – 1941)[48]

Thomas Kelly was born on a farm in southwestern Ohio in 1893. His parents were active Quakers. At the age of four his father died, leaving his mother to support him and his sister. Six years later his mother would move the family to Wilmington, Ohio in search of better opportunities and education for her children. After high school, Thomas enrolled at Wilmington College where he fell in love with both science and philosophy.

After Wilmington he went on for further study at Haverford College where he would be profoundly impacted by Rufus Jones. From 1914 to 1916 Thomas would teach science at Pickering College in Canada. Throughout this time Thomas continued to develop a hunger for life. Around this time Canadian Friends[49] began to take an interest in Quaker missions in Japan. Attracted to this, Thomas would enroll at Hartford Theological Seminary in 1916 in order to prepare for ministry in the Far East. However, the first World War and his studies seemingly changed his missionary focus, but apparently his love for the Far East never left him.

In 1919, after graduating from seminary, Thomas was offered a teaching post in Bible back at Wilmington College. He would accept the position but not before meeting and marrying Lael Macy. Lael was from a prominent Hartford Seminary family. Thomas served at Wilmington College for about two years before he became restless. Thomas and Lael agreed that it was time for Thomas to

---

48   Information on Thomas Kelly is taken from A Biographical Memoir by Douglas V. Steere in: Thomas R. Kelly, *A Testament of Devotion* (Harper Collins: New York, 1992) pgs. 105-127.

49   Quakers referred to one another as "Friends."

pursue the teaching of philosophy but this would require more schooling. Thomas re-enrolled at Hartford Seminary this time focusing on philosophy. Thomas' vision was upon both Eastern and Western philosophy, never taking his eyes off the Far East. In June 1924 he received his PhD degree.

In 1924 Thomas and Lael were selected to minister in post-war Germany. For fifteen months they devoted themselves to the development of a Quaker spiritual center in Berlin. After this Thomas' life seemed to shift quite regularly. He was sought by numerous colleges and universities, often switching teaching posts after just a few short years. All the while, Thomas still desired to experience the Far East, but this was always held off. Also, in the mid-1930's Thomas' health would begin to decline, most likely as a result of his deep devotion to scholarship at the time. It is said that during one lengthy time period he only got out of bed to go to class. He would ultimately succumb to a heart attack at the age of 47 in 1941.

Throughout his life, those who knew him remember him as boisterous, alive, always the life of the party, so to speak. It seems wherever Thomas Kelly went he inspired others. One of the focal points for Thomas was the Presence of God. Our reading selections for this week are taken from *A Testament of Devotion* by Thomas R. Kelly.

WEEK 12, DAY 2

The Light Within

Deep within us all there is an amazing inner sanctuary of the soul, a holy place, a Divine Center, a speaking Voice, to which we may continuously return. Eternity is at our hearts, pressing upon our time-torn lives, warming us with intimations of an astounding destiny, calling us home unto Itself. Yielding to these persuasions, gladly committing ourselves in body and soul, utterly and completely, to the Light Within, is the beginning of true life.

John 1:9; 8:12

The true light that gives light to everyone was coming into the world....When Jesus spoke again to the people, he said, "I am the light of the world. Whoever follows me will never walk in darkness, but will have the light of life."

WEEK 12, DAY 3

Holy Obedience

It is to one strand in this inner drama, one scene, where the Shepherd has found His sheep, that I would direct you. It is the life of absolute and complete and holy obedience to the voice of the Shepherd. But ever throughout the account the accent will be laid upon God, God the initiator, God the aggressor, God the seeker, God the stirrer into life, God the ground of our obedience, God the giver of the power to become children of God.

John 10:1-5

"Very truly I tell you Pharisees, anyone who does not enter the sheep pen by the gate, but climbs in by some other way, is a thief and a robber. The one who enters by the gate is the shepherd of the sheep. The gatekeeper opens the gate for him, and the sheep listen to his voice. He calls his own sheep by name and leads them out. When he has brought out all his own, he goes on ahead of them, and his sheep follow him because they know his voice. But they will never follow a stranger; in fact, they will run away from him because they do not recognize a stranger's voice."

WEEK 12, DAY 4

The Blessed Community

The final grounds of holy Fellowship are in God. Live immersed and drowned in God are drowned in love, and know one another in Him, and know one another in love. God is the medium, the matrix, the focus, the solvent. As Meister Eckhart suggests, he who is wholly surrounded by God, enveloped by God, clothed with God, glowing in selfless love toward Him—such a man no one can touch except he touch God also. Such lives have a common meeting point; they live in a common joyous enslavement. They go back into a single Center where they are at home with Him and with one another.

1 John 1:2-4

The life appeared; we have seen it and testify to it, and we proclaim to you the eternal life, which was with the Father and has appeared to us. We proclaim to you what we have seen and heard, so that you also may have fellowship with us. And our fellowship is with the Father and with his Son, Jesus Christ. We write this to make our joy complete.

WEEK 12, DAY 5

The Eternal Now and Social Concern

There is an experience of the eternal breaking into time, which transforms all life into a miracle of faith and action. Unspeakable, profound, and full of glory as an inward experience, it is the root of concern for all creation, the true ground of social endeavor. This inward Life and the outward Concern are truly one whole, and, were it possible, ought to be described simultaneously.

James 1:22-27

Do not merely listen to the word, and so deceive yourselves. Do what it says.

Anyone who listens to the word but does not do what it says is like someone who looks at his face in a mirror and, after looking at himself, goes away and immediately forgets what he looks like. But whoever looks intently into the perfect law that gives freedom, and continues in it—not forgetting what they have heard, but doing it—they will be blessed in what they do. Those who consider themselves religious and yet do not keep a tight rein on their tongues deceive themselves, and their religion is worthless. Religion that God our Father accepts as pure and faultless is this: to look after orphans and widows in their distress and to keep oneself from being polluted by the world.

WEEK 12, DAY 6

The Simplification of Life

We Western peoples are apt to think our problems are external, environmental. We are not skilled in the inner life, where the real roots of our problem lie. For I would suggest that the true explanation of the complexity of our program is an inner one, not an outer one. The outer distractions of our interests reflect an inner lack of integration of our own lives. We are trying to be several selves at once, without all our selves being organized by a single, mastering Life within us. Each of us tends to be, not a single self, but a whole committee of selves.

Psalm 131:1-2; Matthew 6:31-34

My heart is not proud, Lord, my eyes are not haughty; I do not concern myself with great matters or things too wonderful for me. But I have calmed and quieted myself, I am like a weaned child with its mother; like a weaned child I am content...." "So do not worry, saying, 'What shall we eat?' or 'What shall we drink?' or 'What shall we wear?' For the pagans run after all these things, and your heavenly Father knows that you need them. But seek first his kingdom and his righteousness, and all these things will be given to you as well. Therefore do not worry about tomorrow, for tomorrow will worry about itself. Each day has enough trouble of its own."

WEEK 12, DAY 7

APPLICATION QUESTIONS:

1. Have you ever felt God's Presence? What was happening at that time? Take time to thank God for that experience through prayer.
2. Do you remember when you first embraced the Light of Life? How have you changed and grown since then? In what specific area of your life do you still need to grow?
3. Do you think Church programs are an indication of discontentment? If so, how can the local Church address this issue in our busy, overscheduled society?

SAINT THERESE OF LISIEUX (1873-1897)[50]

While the life of Therese was brief, ending at 24 years of age, the impact of her short life has left a precious legacy. Therese was born in Alencon in Normandy, France on January 2, 1873. She was the youngest of nine children but only five of them would live to their adult years. Four of the five would become Carmelite nuns at Lisieux. The death of her mother in 1877 would have a profound effect upon Therese. For the next nine years she would experience bouts of depression as well as other symptoms. It was during these years that Therese began to develop a desire to become a Carmelite nun. She was granted the opportunity just a few months shy of her fifteenth birthday.

In the year 1893 she began to develop symptoms of tuberculosis. Following this, her health took the trajectory of gradual decline. In the period of four short years Therese would be moved to the Carmelite infirmary. Therese would pass on to glory on September 30th, 1897.

Even though her time on earth was short, one of the endearing and longstanding influences we glean from Therese is known as "the little way." Therese often spoke of a desire to remain as a little child before the Lord, remaining humble and in constant need of Christ's love, grace, and presence. John Nelson describes the five elements of Therese's "little way" as follows:[51]

---

50 Information for the introduction to Therese of Lisieux is taken from Louise Dupre and James A. Wiseman, *Light from Light: An Anthology of Christian Mysticism* (Paulist Press; New York, 2001), pgs. 412-416.

51 John Nelson, *The Little Way of Saint Therese of Lisieux: Into the Arms of Love* (Ligouri Publications; Ligouri, Missouri, 1997), pg. 2.

1. Joyful humility as a little child of God.
2. Bold confidence in God's mercy and loving-kindness.
3. Tranquil trust in the actions of God's limitless love.
4. Persistence in prayer as a simple raising of the heart to God.
5. Daily practice of the little way of love.

The following references to Therese of Lisieux's work are taken from John Nelson's *The Little Way of Saint Therese of Lisieux: Into the Arms of Love.*

WEEK 13, DAY 2

From a letter to Celine, July 6, 1893

It is Jesus who does everything in me; I do nothing except remain little and weak

John 15:5

"I am the vine, you are the branches. If you remain in me and I in you, you will bear much fruit; apart from me you can do nothing.

WEEK 13, DAY 3

Letter to Celine, April 25, 1893

To be His, one must be small, small as a drop of dew! Oh! how few souls there are that aspire to stay so small. "But," say they, "the river and the brook are surely more useful than the dewdrop? What does it do? It is good for nothing, save to give a few moments' refreshment to a flower of the fields which is today and tomorrow is no more."

They are right, of course: the dewdrop is good for no more than that; but they do not know the wild Flower which has chosen to dwell in our land of exile and remain here during the short night of His life. If they knew it, they would understand the rebuke Jesus gave Martha long ago (Luke 10:41). Our Beloved has no need for our fine thoughts—has He not His angels, His legions of heavenly spirits, whose knowledge infinitely surpasses that of the greatest geniuses of our sad earth?

So it is not intellect or talents that Jesus has come upon earth to seek. He became the Flower of the fields solely to show us how He loves simplicity....What a privilege to be called to so high a mission!...but to respond to it how simple one must remain.

Matthew 5:3, 5

"Blessed are the poor in spirit, for theirs is the kingdom of heaven....Blessed are the meek, for they will inherit the earth."

Week 13, Day 4

The Story of a Soul, VIII, 105

Whenever I open a book, no matter how beautiful or touching, my heart dries up and I can understand nothing of what I read; or if I do understand, my mind will go no further, and I cannot meditate. I am rescued from this helpless state by the Scriptures and the Imitation, finding in them a hidden manna, pure and substantial; but during meditation I am sustained above all else by the Gospels. They supply my poor soul's every need, and they are always yielding up to me new lights and mysterious hidden meanings. I know from experience that "the Kingdom of God is within us" (Luke 17:21), and that Jesus has no need of books or doctors to instruct our soul; He the Doctor of Doctors, teaches us without the sound of words. I have never heard Him speak, and yet I know He is within my soul. Every moment His is guiding and inspiring me, and just at the moment I need them, "lights" till then unseen are granted me. Most often it is not at prayer that they come but while I go about my daily duties.

Psalm 119:105-107

Your word is a lamp for my feet,
a light for my path.
I have taken an oath and confirmed it,
that I will follow your righteous laws.
I have suffered much;
preserve my life, Lord,
according to your word.

WEEK 13, DAY 5

Said to Mother Agnes of Jesus, August 7, 1897

If I were to say to myself: I have acquired a certain virtue, and I am certain I can practice it....this would be relying upon my own strength, and when we do this, we run the risk of falling into the abyss. However, I will have the right of doing stupid things up until my death, if I am humble and if I remain little. Look at little children: they never stop breaking things, tearing things, falling down, and they do this even while loving their parents very, very much. When I fall in this way, it makes me realize my nothingness more, and I say to myself: What would I do, and what would I become, if I were to rely upon my own strength?

Matthew 19:13-15

Then people brought little children to Jesus for him to place his hands on them and pray for them. But the disciples rebuked him.

Jesus said, "Let the little children come to me, and do not hinder them, for the kingdom of heaven belongs to such as these." When he had placed his hands on them, he went on from there.

Week 13, Day 6

The Story of a Soul, X, 141

For a long time I had to kneel during meditation near a Sister who could not stop fidgeting; if it was not with her Rosary, it was with goodness knows what else. Maybe no one else noticed it; I have a very sensitive ear. But you have no idea how much it annoyed me. I wanted to turn around and glare at the culprit to make her be quiet, but deep in my heart I felt the best thing to do was to put up with it patiently for the love of God first of all, and also not to hurt her feelings. So I kept quiet, bathed in perspiration often enough, while my prayer was nothing more than the prayer of suffering! In the end I tried to find some way of bearing it peacefully and joyfully, at least in my inmost heart; then I even tried to like this wretched little noise.

It was impossible not to hear it, so I turned my whole attention to listening really closely to it as if it were a magnificent concert, and spent the rest of the time offering it to Jesus. It was certainly not the prayer of quiet!

Romans 12:9-12

Love must be sincere. Hate what is evil; cling to what is good. Be devoted to one another in love. Honor one another above yourselves. Never be lacking in zeal, but keep your spiritual fervor, serving the Lord. Be joyful in hope, patient in affliction, faithful in prayer.

WEEK 13, DAY 7

APPLICATION QUESTIONS:

1. Therese of Lisieux provides is with a healthy counterbalance to our current cultural situation. In our day and age of social media, celebrity and status, Therese shows us the way of humility, littleness, love and grace. How is Therese's life a challenge to you in this regard?
2. Therese of Lisieux often referred to herself as a helpless child before the Lord. When you think of a child, what are some of the images that come to your mind? How could you possibly embrace a more child-like faith?
3. Although Therese's life was very short, she shows us a life of sacrifice. Rather than needlessly offend a Sister, she was able to turn a distraction into a spiritual discipline. How could you embrace this example in your daily life? Is there a specific task that you regularly are called to do that you could turn into a spiritual discipline?

Appendix A – Spiritual Direction

Spiritual Direction is another form of discipleship or walking the Christian journey with another mature believer. As the reader was encouraged in the beginning of this book to walk this journey in community, utilizing the guidance of a spiritual director can be a very helpful addition to following Christ. The description below is taken from Kenneth Boa, *Conformed to His Image: Biblical and Practical Approaches to Spiritual Formation* (Zondervan: Grand Rapids, 2001) pg. 440.

Until recently, Protestants have thought little about the ancient art of spiritual direction,… More people are becoming aware of the benefits of this form of pastoral care that focuses on the cultivation of prayer, discernment, and practical implementation of spiritual truth.

In the early centuries of the church, spiritual direction was associated with desert monasticism and continued to develop within monastic contexts as a means of providing intensive personal guidance. As "physicians of the soul" who help people understand the workings of God in their lives, spiritual directors must be people of wisdom, depth, skill, and prayer. To be effective in this form of soul care, they must be marked by a combination of *knowledge*, (Scripture, spiritual classics and spiritual theology, psychology, the nature and machinations of the psyche), *discernment*, (the ability to perceive the nature of souls, sensitivity to the difference between the work of the Spirit and the work of the flesh/or false spirits), and *character* (vitality in faith and prayer, holiness of life, humility and brokenness through personal suffering, loving concern, openness to the ministry of the Spirit).

Spiritual directors help people discern the workings of grace in their lives and offer them guidance and assistance as they seek to progress in prayer and obedience. Their relationship with those who seek their ministry is not authoritarian or that of a professional service (e.g., the counselor-client model) but as companions on the spiritual journey who enhance inner desire and clarify the movement of the Spirit. They care for the soul through cleansing, discernment, clarification, alignment, and implementation.

Such directors must be sought out, but it is not easy to find them. When we do, we should not expect them to flatter us or cater to our illusions. Instead, we must approach them in a spirit of humility and let them know what we think, feel, and desire. Good directors will ask appropriate questions, listen skillfully, reveal barriers to growth, assist in confession and repentance, show how to listen to God and how to implement spiritual disciplines, rebuke and encourage as necessary, and offer their presence and compassion. Spiritual directors have skill in distinguishing between spiritual and psychological problems (e.g., spiritual aridity versus psychosomatic illness or infantile moodiness).

Appendix B – Lectio Divina and The Prayer of Examen

There are various methods of prayer that have been cultivated and utilized over the centuries. Two examples of these are lectio divina and the prayer of examen.

Lectio Divina

This description is taken from Kennth Boa, *Conformed to His Image: Biblical and Practical Approaches to Spiritual Formation* (Zondervan: Grand Rapids, 2001), pg. 96.

The ancient art of *lectio divina*, or sacred reading, was introduced to the West by the Eastern desert father John Cassian early in the fifth century. It has been practiced for centuries by Cistercian monks…and is being rediscovered in wider parts of the Christian community. This extraordinarily beneficial approach combines the disciplines of study, prayer, and meditation into a powerful method that, when it is consistently applied, can revolutionize one's spiritual life. Sacred reading consists of four elements.

1. *Lectio* (reading). Select a very short text and ingest it by reading it several times. I normally chose a verse or a brief passage from the chapters I read from the Old and New Testaments in my morning Bible reading.
2. *Meditatio* (meditation). Take a few minutes to reflect on the words and phrases and phrases in the text you have read. Ponder the passage by asking questions and using your imagination.
3. *Oratio* (prayer). Having internalized the passage, offer it back to God in the form of personalized prayer.

4. *Contemplatio* (comtemplation). For most of us, this will be the most difficult part, since it consists of silence and yieldedness in the presence of God. Contemplation is the fruit of the dialogue of the first three elements; it is the communion that is born out of our reception of divine truth in our minds and hearts.

THE PRAYER OF EXAMEN

The practice of the prayer of examen was developed by St. Ignatius of Loyola in the 16th century. Ignatius was one of the founders of the Society of Jesus, also known as the Jesuits. The following description of the prayer of examen is taken from the Ignatian Spirituality website: https://www.ignatianspirituality.com/ignatian-prayer/the-examen/

The Daily Examen is a technique of prayerful reflection on the events of the day in order to detect God's presence and discern his direction for us. The Examen is an ancient practice in the Church that can help us see God's hand at work in our whole experience.

The method presented here is adapted from a technique described by Ignatius Loyola in his Spiritual Exercises. St. Ignatius thought that the Examen was a gift that came directly from God, and that God wanted it to be shared as widely as possible. One of the few rules of prayer that Ignatius made for the Jesuit order was the requirement that Jesuits practice the Examen twice daily—at noon and at the end of the day. It's a habit that Jesuits, and many other Christians, practice to this day.

This is a version of the five-step Daily Examen that St. Ignatius practiced.

1. Become aware of God's presence.
2. Review the day with gratitude.
3. Pay attention to your emotions.
4. Choose one feature of the day and pray from it.
5. Look toward tomorrow.

ACKNOWLEDGMENTS

Once again, I'm reminded of the axiom that everything we do is connected to those who have gone before us in some manner. Writing a book, any genre of book, is no different. In light of this, I'd like to thank Dr. Laurie Mellinger. Dr. Mellinger is responsible for introducing me to the great cloud of witnesses who have gone before us, paving the way for the rest of us. I'm forever grateful to her for opening that door and showing me what I've been missing. Also, Dr. H. Douglas Buckwalter deserves much credit for always encouraging me to stay focused on Jesus Christ, as well as encouraging me to continue the practice of writing. I wouldn't be who I am today in many ways without his encouragement and friendship.

I must acknowledge, with deep respect and gratitude, Henry Neufeld from Energion Publications for welcoming me and allowing this work to see the light of day. This is my second time working with Henry and Energion and it is once again a true pleasure and a blessing. Furthermore, I must acknowledge Chris Eyre, Henry's right-hand man and a wonderful editor. Thank you for cleaning up my messes and for your keen and careful eyes. It is editors like yourself who make writers look and sound like we know what we are saying. Any mistakes in this work are entirely of my own making, no one else is responsible.

Last, but certainly not least, I'm indebted to my amazing family, my wife Stacey, and my daughters, Emma and Ana. The three of you are my greatest gift and blessing. You make me a better person and encourage me to continue to walk in the way of Jesus. You forever have my heart.

BIBLIOGRAPHY AND FURTHER READING

à Kempis, Thomas. *The Imitation of Christ.* Ed. Paul Bechtel. Chicago: Moody Press, 1980.

Aelred of Rievalux. *Spiritual Friendship.* Allen, TX: Christian Classics, 2008.

Benedict, Saint. *The Rule of Saint Benedict.* Available from http://www.ccel.org/ccel/benedict/rule.i.html?highlight=benedict#highlight.

Boa, Kenneth. *Conformed to His Image: Biblical and Practical Approaches to Spiritual Formation.* Zondervan: Grand Rapids, 2001.

Bonaventure. *The Soul's Journey into God; The Tree of Life; The Life of St. Francis.* Translated by Ewert Cousins. New York: Paulist Press, 1978.

Brother Lawrence. *The Practice of the Presence of God.* Grand Rapids: Revell, 1999.

Calvin, John. "Of Prayer—A Perpetual Exercise of Faith." Available from http://www.ccel.org/ccel/calvin/prayer.html.

Dupré, Louis, and James A. Wiseman, eds. *Light from Light: An Anthology of Christian Mysticism.* 2nd edition. Mahwah, NJ: Paulist Press, 2001.

John of the Cross: *Selected Writings.* Edited and introduced by Kieran Kavanaugh. New York: Paulist Press, 1987.

Julian of Norwich, *Revelations of Divine Love.* Translated by Elizabeth Spearing. New York: Penguin Classics, 1999.

Kelly, Thomas R. *A Testament of Devotion.* New York: HarperOne, 1996.

Luther, Martin. "A Simple Way to Pray." Available from www.
    hope-aurora.org/docs/ ASimpleWaytoPray.pdf. (Also in *Lu-
    ther's Works*, vol. 43 [Devotional Writings II]: 193-211.)

Merton, Thomas. *Wisdom of the Desert: Sayings of the Desert Fathers
    of the Fourth Century.* Boston: Shambhala Publications, 2004.

Nelson, John. *The Little Way of Saint Therese of Lisieux: Into the
    Arms of Love.* Liguori, Missouri: Liguori Publications, 1997.

Way of a Pilgrim. Translated by Olga Savin. Boston: Shambhala
    Publications, 2001.

Wesley, John. *A Plain Account of Christian Perfection.* Kansas City,
    MO: Beacon Hill Press, 2000.

Woods, Richard J. *Christian Spirituality: God's Presence Through the
    Ages.* Expanded edition. Maryknoll, NY: Orbis Books, 2006.

https://www.ignatianspirituality.com/ignatian-prayer/the-examen/